*A NEW ENGLISH GRAMMAR

*A NEW ENGLISH
GRAMMAR

JEFF DOLVEN

Praise for *A New English Grammar*:

In Wittgenstein's later writing, he proves the dependence
of grammar on context. The strangest sentences make
sudden sense in the right context, while the most familiar
phrases—on investigation—sound suddenly strange. *A New
English Grammar* undertakes the same transformation in a
lyric context. "Grammar tells what kind of object anything
is," Wittgenstein proposes, and here it tells us the object is
poetry. For the philosopher, being alert to grammar saves
us from being misled into error; for the poet, it seduces us
into reverie. "Not empiricism and yet realism in philosophy,"
Wittgenstein learned, "is the hardest thing." The same could
be said for poetry, and Dolven makes it look easy.

—Craig Dworkin

A philosophical poetics, an excursus and dithyramb, a rid-
dling undoing of rule and prescribed rightness, Jeff Dolven's
A New English Grammar swims deep into beautifully dis-
tressed, surprising waters. I was about to about to about
to about to say it is unlike anything else, and I am saying
it. Dolven has the peculiar capacity to rewire your brain.
"A-wandering somewhere" and a wondering through and
with grammar, this book shows how error spurs the poet's
errand, grammar births lyric glamour, and the apparently
wrong sponsors a new kind of song. This is brilliant mind-
fuckery and tender art.

—Maureen N. McLane

CONTENTS

INTRODUCTION

There is a proof in set theory showing that the set of natural numbers, though it is infinite, is nonetheless smaller than the infinite set of real numbers. You can count one-by-one as high as you like, you never need to stop, but between each rung of your number-ladder is another infinity of fractional differences. Might the same be said of sentences? It is a premise of transformational grammar that the number of correct sentences to be made by applying the existing rules to the available vocabulary is infinite. But if you understand each one of those correct sentences to have a limitless number of incorrect, ungrammatical counterparts—generated by a misplaced preposition, a confusion of tenses, a disagreement of number—surely that second set is larger. There are infinite ways to get it right, but even more ways to get it wrong.

The linguists' symbol for a faulty sentence (or clause or phrase or word-form) is an asterisk: *He had had gone. That asterisk is not used to call out a mistake in the wild, but to indicate an example that has, in its wrongness, in its breach of usage and of the rules that codify usage, something to teach us. *Study this*, says the asterisk, *but do not talk this way*. The choice of that stylized six-pointed star nonetheless suggests—if you allow it to signify beyond the linguists' formalisms—that there is more to the story. Asterisks qualify: a claim that comes with an asterisk may be taken back elsewhere. Or they complicate: there is an aside, or a second thought, waiting at the bottom of the page. The symbol also has a technical use in the field of conversational analysis, where it denotes an instance of what is called "conversational repair." Such repair is something speakers do all the time, and grammar accounts for only a subset of the possible reasons; we might get a date wrong, or find a better word, or mispell, *misspell, something in a text message. The asterisk signifies that what comes next is a revision in real time, going back to a previous utterance to fix it.

What if we did not go back, but went forward? Not, that is, corrected the mistake, or flagged it for study, or for shame, but proceeded as though it were no mistake—as though it were meaningful, and implied rules that might be trusted in language at large? Or even, as though it were the revelation, or the birth, of a new language? That would be to treat the counterexample as a counterfactual, a small, sub-junctive gesture toward a different world, different because a linguistic glitch here is idiomatic there. The asterisk invites a step forward into that world. It is the first star of that new sky. From that new vantage, the vantage of a new English grammar, what could we see about the world we used to live in? What would have to change, about our beliefs, our customs, our politics, for the new sentence to be correct? Why ever was it not? Perfectly correct sentences have the power to make new worlds, even infinite new worlds, and perhaps, in a small way, every correct sentence does just that. But there are more infinities open to us.

*TENSE

Traditional grammar usually presents English as having a future tense, namely the form using the auxiliary verb *will*. There are two directions in which one could object to this analysis. First, the auxiliary *will* has a number of other uses. Second, there are many instances of future time reference where it is not necessary to use the auxiliary *will*, but where rather the so-called present tense suffices. In some subordinate clauses, the auxiliary *will* with reference to future time is excluded, even if it would be required in a main clause. So, in a main clause:

1a.   *It will rain tomorrow.*
1b.   **It rains tomorrow.*

But in a subordinate clause, depending on the main:

2a.   *If it rains tomorrow, we will get wet.*
2b.   **If it will rain tomorrow, we will get wet.*

On the other hand, in conditional (or *if*) clauses that do not refer to a specific time, *will* with a modal meaning (expressing necessity or probability) is permitted, e.g., *if he will go swimming in dangerous waters, he will drown*. Thus it is clear that in such subordinate clauses, future time reference uses of *will*, which are excluded, are grammatically distinct from modal uses of *will*, which are allowed. These examples therefore suggest (but do not, of course, prove) that English does have a future tense, and hence a structural capacity to distinguish between what will happen, what might happen, and what we want to happen, even if speakers themselves cannot.

If it will rain tomorrow, then
today it will rain, without a doubt,
which does not prove the contrary

though we can always pray it will:
will rain tomorrow, that's to say,
as sure as anything under the sun

it will, and in the meantime we'll
keep tossing the basin into the air.
Someone will will the water to rain.

Grammatical compositionality is the principle that the meaning of an expression is determined by the meaning of its parts and their method of composition. The *formes supercomposées* in French are dependent on exploiting the possibilities of compositionality one step further than is done in English, where *he had had gone* is not possible. Even in French, however, the compositionality is not recursive:

1.   *il avait eu rassemblé*
2.   **il avait eu eu rassemblé*

This is one way in which constructions such as the pluperfect *had* differ from periphrastic constructions like English *to be about to, to have just,* which can be combined recursively to give formally impeccable combinations (*I was about to about to about to about to go*), even if it is difficult to compute their meanings or find a self-respecting use for them.

He had had gone. The door slammed twice.
Thinking again? Or doubling down?
It slammed again when we said it again.

Most of our doors swing out and in,
though sometimes it takes a little push.
Others are one-way, interior valves.

Then there are doors that only open
once, and can never be shut again.
May we come and go as we please O please.

In distinguishing between the grammatical status of states and occurrences, the first contrast is between static and dynamic situations. States exist or obtain, while occurrences happen or take place. Occurrences involve change, while states do not. States have no internal temporal structure: they are the same throughout their history. The distinction between the two main types of situation is reflected linguistically in the difference between the simple present and the progressive aspect. The simple present combines freely with states but not with occurrences.

1a.	*The flag was red.*	[state]
1b.	*The flag is red.*	[state]
2a.	*She married Tom.*	[occurrence]
2b.	**She marries Tom.*	[occurrence]

While [1b] is the present time counterpart of [1a], [2b] resists a comparable interpretation—it can hardly be used for an event that is actually taking place at the time of speaking. The progressive aspect, using the auxiliary *be* to express an ongoing action or situation, does not normally occur with expressions denoting states:

3.	*He is playing tennis.*	[occurrence]
4.	**The flag is being red.*	[state]

The flag is being red again.
Red with anger, there's reason to fear,
unless it's only saying stop

and frisk with me in the meadows, friend,
or blushing, wrapped around itself
to hide somebody's nakedness.

Look how it waves away our concerns.
It's only red like the poor are being
poor, not like the rich are rich.

Achievements are conceived of as punctual, i.e., as being instantaneous, occurring at a point in time, whereas processes—like states—are conceived of as durative, as having duration. The two kinds of process, accomplishments and activities, are distinguished by the fact that the former are telic: they have an inherent terminal point beyond which they cannot continue. Activities (and states) are atelic. Writing or reading some particular letter or note, walking some specific distance (*We walked six kilometers*) or to some specific destination (*We walked to the post office*) are accomplishments. Once we have covered six kilometers, the situation of our walking six kilometers is necessarily terminated: we can carry on walking (for that is an activity), but not walking six kilometers.

Both kinds of processes occur freely with progressive aspect, whereas punctual achievements tend to resist it:

1a.   *I was working.*   [activity]
1b.   *I was writing a novel.*   [accomplishment]
1c.   *I was recognizing her.*   [achievement]

A complication arises with verbs like *die*.

I was recognizing her, and then
there must have been a change of light.
I had to start all over again.

I had to start all over again,
both of us holding perfectly still,
but was that a smile, and if so, whose?

I was so close!—If only I'd glimpsed
the telltale scar that marks where we
were amputated, and from what.

Verbs like *die* behave as achievement expressions, and there-fore—unlike accomplishments and activities—they do not readily occur with aspectual verbs like *begin* or *finish*. Compare *He finished painting the house last week* (accom-plishment) and **He finished dying last week* (achievement). Nevertheless, such verbs occur quite freely in the progress-ive: *He was dying*. This usage of course has a durative rather than a punctual interpretation, and we will therefore refer to situations expressed by *die* and the like as "extendable achievements," in contrast to "strict achievements."

The admissibility and interpretation of expressions of duration differentiate among the three kinds of dynamic situation, achievement (which is punctual), activity (which is indefinitely extended), and accomplishment (which has duration, but is limited by other factors).

1a.   **He reached the summit for an hour.*   [achievement]
1b.   **He was dying for an hour.*   [extendable achievement]
1c.   *He played tennis for an hour / *in an hour.*   [activity]
1d.   *He walked a mile in an hour /*
        *for an hour.   [accomplishment]
2a.   *It took him an hour to reach the summit / die.*   [achievement]
2b.   **It took him an hour to play tennis.*   [activity]
2c.   *It took him an hour to walk a mile.*   [accomplishment]

The grammar is indifferent as to whether hurry or delay is to be preferred.

He was dying for an hour,
then he died. He was dying
for an hour of not dying,

it didn't matter to him which.
He was dying for an hour,
one special hour, hours ago,

he'd know it again if it came again.
He was dying for an hour,
dying to do it again, and again.

*AGREEMENT

Either requires a count singular noun: *either parent,* but not **either children* (children being plural) or **either information* (*information* being a non-count noun; it does not form the plural **informations*). Like *any, either* has both a non-affirmative use (*either*$_n$) and a free choice use (*either*$_f$).

1a.   *He didn't like either*$_n$ *teacher.*
1b.   **He liked either teacher.*
2a.   *Did either*$_n$ *boy have a key?*
2b.   **Either boy has a key.*
3a.   *You can choose either*$_f$ *door.*
3b.   **She had chosen either door.*

The inadmissible [b] examples are affirmative and also exclude a free choice interpretation, as is obvious in [3b]: the choice of doors is no longer free once the choice has been made.

Either boy has a key, the host explains.
The contestants get to make a choice
of either one, but had best choose fast.

The keys' teeth bite the boys' soft palms
like the fox hid under the Spartan's shirt.
The boys are strong and give no sign.

Which will be which, when all is known?
The contestants have nothing to lose, it seems.
But both of the boys have different keys.

While *either* is often used in statements posing alternatives, it is excluded from such questions if there is no alternative to the given alternatives.

1. *They are coming on either Monday or Tuesday.*
2. *Are they coming on either Monday or Tuesday?*
3. *Are you either coming or not?*

Example [2] can only be a polar question, one with *Yes* and *No* answers: yes, they are coming on one of those two days, or no, they are coming on another day, or not coming at all. Example [3] is simply inadmissible. The admissibility of a sentence such as ?*Are you either alive or dead* will depend on whether a third possibility is understood.

Are you either coming or not,
or not? Please check one box or two.
Be honest. There's only one wrong answer.

Be sure to use both sides of your pencil.
The boxes are larger than you think,
and often placed on top of each other,

and truth be told they have no bottom.
Be sure to fill them in completely.
Feel free to use all sides of the page.

There are a great number of dual-transitivity verbs in English, verbs which occur in both transitive and intransitive constructions, i.e., with and without direct objects—such verbs greatly outnumber those that are restricted to just one or other of the two constructions. The object of such dual-transitivity verbs may sometimes be optionally stated, as *court, divorce, embrace, kiss, marry, cross, touch,* or *meet,* but is mandatory for **help, *love, *resemble,* or **betray.*

1a.   *They kissed (each other) passionately.*
1b.   *The lines cross (each other) here.*
2a.   *They resemble each other closely.*
2b.   ** They resemble closely.*

Some verbs are always semantically symmetrical: *Kim married Pat,* for example, entails *Pat married Kim* (for the primary sense of marry). But generally reciprocity is merely common rather than necessary. For example, *Kim kissed Pat* very clearly does not entail *Pat kissed Kim,* as the one kissed can be entirely passive (and can indeed be inanimate: *Kim kissed the cross*). Nor does *Kim divorced Pat* entail *Pat divorced Kim,* since it involves Kim initiating the proceedings; nor *Kim betrayed Pat,* nor *Pat betrayed the cause,* and so on. Again, the intransitive versions tend to be commoner than the reciprocal transitives, whether or not the feeling is mutual.

They resemble closely: side
by side, who could tell them apart?
Eye for eye, and tooth for tooth,

identical, symmetrical;
left for right, and hemisphere
for hemisphere. It's going to take

two rooms, just past security,
two separate, sound-proof rooms, where one
or the other is free to betray themselves.

In general a subject that coordinates two or more noun phrases linked by *and* takes a plural verb, as in *Mary and John are here*, etc. There are several constructions, however, where the verb is singular. One case is seen in:

1.   [*Eggs and bacon*] _is_ / *_are_ my favorite breakfast.
2.   [*The hammer and sickle*] _was_ / *_were_ flying over the Kremlin.
3.   [*Your laziness and your ineptitude*] _amazes_ / _amaze_ me.

Such examples can be regarded as involving a singular override similar to that found with measure phrases: the subject is conceptualized as a single unit and this determines the singular verb. In [1] the predicative *my favorite breakfast* can only apply to eggs and bacon as a unit, and hence a plural verb is impossible. If we change the predicative to, say, *good for you*, both singular and plural verbs are possible, but with a difference of meaning. In *Eggs and bacon is good for you* the subject is again conceptualized as a single unit (a meal consisting of eggs and bacon), whereas in *Eggs and bacon are good for you* the two foods are separately good for you. In [2] the coordination is between two nouns rather than two noun phrases, but again we have a unitary conceptualization: the subject refers to a flag. In [3] both singular and plural verbs are possible, the singular conveying that the laziness and ineptitude form a single cause of amazement, the plural conveying that each of them is a cause of amazement. The choice between singular and plural conceptualizations is more readily available with abstract noun phrases than with concrete noun phrases: compare, for example, *John and his father amazes me*.

John and his father amazes me,
how he was inside his head and then
rode out and happily ever after.

How everything came with him, too.
The patents, the horse and the cart, the deeds
amazes me and more and more

amazes me as and and where
it came from, father, son, and I
forget if there was anyone else.

Exclamative *what* modifies only noun phrases (*what a difficult problem*), whereas exclamative *how* modifies adjectives, degree determinatives, adverbs, and verbs (*how difficult a problem*, etc.). *How* does not function immediately in noun phrase structure, but phrases containing it can nonetheless occur with count singular nouns. Compare the following exclamative phrases, which might occur in such a frame as " ___ *we have on our hands!*"

1a.	*what a difficult problem*	[count singular]
1b.	*how difficult a problem*	
2a.	*what difficult problems*	[plural]
2b.	**how difficult problems*	
3a.	*what difficult work*	[non-count]
3b.	**how difficult work*	

So resembles *how* in that it can modify an attributive adjective only in count singular noun phrases with following *a*, while *such* occurs in the three main kinds of noun phrase, as *what* does. The following therefore match the examples above, but would not be fronted in the sentence, so that they might occur in the frame "*We have ___ on our hands!*":

4a.	*such a difficult problem*	[count singular]
4b.	*so difficult a problem*	
5a.	*such difficult problems*	[plural]
5b.	**so difficult problems*	
6a.	*such difficult work*	[non-count]
6b.	**so difficult work*	

How so however is not for a grammar to answer.

How difficult problems. How difficult work.
How to begin, friend, after too long?
So great a distance. How strong a thirst

for such and such a syllable:
laid up in salt and carried through customs,
it gets there as dry as a period.

So difficult problems. How do you say
a glass of water for my friend?
How to my friend? So difficult work.

*CASE AND NUMBER

The choice among the different cases of the personal pronouns—nominative (subject), accusative (object), and genitive (possessive)—depends on the function of the pronoun in the construction containing it. The choice between reflexive and non-reflexive forms depends primarily on the structural relationship between the pronoun and its antecedent. There are three possibilities for the reflexive: mandatory, optional, and inadmissible.

1.   *Anne blames <u>herself</u> / *<u>her</u> for the accident.*   [mandatory]
2.   *<u>Anne</u> tied a rope around <u>herself</u> / <u>her</u>.*   [optional]
3.   *<u>Anne</u> realizes that they blame *<u>herself</u> / <u>her</u>*
      for the accident.   [inadmissible]

Broadly speaking, reflexives are used when there is a strong structural relation between pronoun and antecedent, as (ideally) between *yourself* and *you*. The same is true where the pronoun is related to the verb not directly but via a preposition: a reflexive may have any of the three statuses we have defined, mandatory, optional, or inadmissible. These are illustrated in 4–6 respectively:

4a.   *<u>He</u> was beside <u>himself</u> with anger.*
4b.   *<u>He</u> was beside <u>him</u> with anger.*
5a.   *<u>Liz</u> wrapped the rug around <u>herself</u>.*
5b.   *<u>Liz</u> wrapped the rug around <u>her</u>.*
6a.   *<u>I</u> haven't any money on <u>myself</u>.*
6b.   *<u>I</u> haven't any money on <u>me</u>.*

I haven't any money on
myself: my bets are placed elsewhere.
My coin bears someone else's name.

My coin: I place it on my eye,
and I can see the satellite
looking down from its own cool orbit.

It knows myself like I know me.
It spins in the sky, a tossed coin.
All my money is on itself.

One quite large class of plural-only nouns consists of words denoting objects made up of two like parts: we refer to these as bipartites. They include names of optical aids, articles of clothing, and tools, as in *glasses*, *pants*, or *pliers*. It should be noted that there is a restricted use of bipartite nouns as singulars:

1.   *This scissor reportedly never needs sharpening.*
2.   *They're selling a pant with last winter's cut.*
3.   *He developed a binocular of especially fine regard.*

Examples like these are most likely to be encountered in the language of commerce or in a historical survey of clothing, tools, and so on. The crucial feature of this usage is that the reference is to types, not to individual specimens. For specimens the plural form is required (*These scissors* / * *This scissor will have to be sharpened*), and it is for this reason that bipartites, however intimate, fall within our definition of plural-only nouns.

This scissor will have to be sharpened, please.
Please leave the other one blunt. The cut
is kindest coming from just one side.

Consider how one parts a loaf
of bread against the cutting board,
or cleaves an apple in the hand,

just as a dancing partner is pressed
against the night, or a soldier finds
himself between the sword and the day.

Other is like *one* in that it inflects (i.e., changes its form) for number, with *others* as the plural form. This establishes quite clearly that it is a noun, to be distinguished from *other*, the adjective. Like the noun *one*, the noun *other* occurs only as the head of a phrase. When we expand to a non-reduced form—from *others* to *the other boxes*—we retain *other*: *the other boxes*. What is retained, however, is not the noun *other* but the lexical base, which is now syntactically an adjective. Note also that although the plural inflection shows that *other* has been converted into a noun, it retains some distributional properties of the adjective *other*, as illustrated in:

1.   *the red other boxes
2.   *the red others

Instead of [1] one says *the other red boxes*: attributive *other* cannot follow an adjective, and the same applies to the noun *other*, except in the case of a true other.

The red other boxes are stocked behind
the red boxes proper, next to the green,
the green other boxes—but for their covers,

the same other boxes, only confused
by customers as colorblind
as everyone is colorblind.

The red other boxes are not to be opened
except in emergencies, like now.
You'll know the ones: they're red right through.

There are three main positions for the subject.

1. *The city had been unusually peaceful.*   [basic position]
2. *Had the city been unusually*
    peaceful?   [post-auxiliary position]
3. *Unusually peaceful had been the city.*   [postposed position]

The basic position is before the main verb. The subject
occurs in post-auxiliary position in the various constructions
involving subject-auxiliary inversion, such as questions, as in
[2]. Finally a subject in postposed position follows the main
verb in final position in the clause; usually there is also a
preposed complement or adjunct in front position, as in [3].
In spite of the importance of position in marking the sub-
ject, it interacts with other factors.

1. *A particular worry was*
    the watchmen.   [complement–main verb–subject]
2. *The following morning came*
    news of her father's arrest.   [auxiliary–main verb–subject]
3. *A loud explosion heard*
    the children.   [object–main verb–subject]

Where *x* is the object, the order *x*–main verb–subject is
excluded, but not for other values of *x*. The ban on object–
main verb–subject reflects the fact that noun phrases in
subject and object function can be of the same semantic type,
so that the meaning of the noun phrases themselves may
give no indication as to which is the subject and which the
object. In *Kim betrays Pat*, for example, there is nothing but
the order to tell us who is the betrayer and who the betrayed.

A loud explosion heard the children,
though everyone else was deafened by it.
Nothing else heard everyone after.

Nothing remembered anyone either,
saving the children, far from the center,
but closer by far to their beginning.

Still they are hearing it ever after.
The last shall be first, and the first shall be last,
and that's just the way it used to be.

The two major uses of adjectives are as attributive modifier in noun phrase structure, and as predicative complement (following a linking verb such as *be*) in clause structure:

1.   *an <u>excellent</u> result*   [attributive modifier]
2.   *The result was <u>excellent</u>.*   [predicative complement]

Most adjectives can occur in both functions, but some are restricted to one or the other. Attributive-only adjectives, which must precede the noun they modify, include the likes of *elder, main,* and *mere.* One group of very clearly non-attributive adjectives comprises those formed with the prefix *a-* that originates in the Middle English preposition *an,* meaning "in, on." For example: *ablaze, aglimmer, alight, asleep, afloat, aglitter, alike, averse, afoot, aglow, alive, awake, afraid, agog, alone, aware, aghast, agleam, ajar, akin, amiss, askew, awash, awry.* Phrases like *a child who was asleep* do not have attributive paraphrases: *an asleep child* is strongly ungrammatical.

An asleep child: where is he going?
A-wandering somewhere we can't go,
toward his rest, but not there yet,

somewhere we can't go, alas,
back before what we assumed,
so sleep, minor premise, sweet a priori,

adrift in the anteroom, little one, sleep;
sleep while your minder holds you against
his chest, his only asymptote.

*GENDER

A significant number of items—specific words, fixed or variable phrases, and idiomatic expressions—are polarity-sensitive, i.e., sensitive to the polarity, positive or negative, of the environment in which they occur. Some items are admissible in negative environments but not normally in positive ones, while others occur in positive environments but generally not in negative ones:

1a.   *She doesn't see him any longer.*
1b.   *She knows him already.*
2a.   **She sees him any longer.*
2b.   **She doesn't know him already.*

Any longer, for example, is acceptable in negative [1a] but not in positive [2a]. And conversely *already* is acceptable in positive [1b] but not in negative [2b] (ignoring the special case when it is used to contradict a previous utterance like [1b]). Items which prefer negative contexts over positive ones (such as *any longer*) are negatively-oriented polarity-sensitive items, or NPIs; items which prefer positive contexts over negative ones (such as *already*) are positively-oriented polarity-sensitive items, or PPIs; and anyone who does not already know as much no longer does not.

She doesn't know him already: half
an hour now, and still the arrow
hangs in the air midway between them;

half a year, now half two years,
already she hardly knows his name,
though the arrow writes it in the air;

already never, and see how the arrow
almost rests its tip on her breast.
A saint's life: a half-life: radiant.

Certain prepositions define contexts for negatively-oriented polarity-sensitive items (NPIs), as illustrated in the following examples:

1a. *She did it without any difficulty.*
1b. **She did it with any difficulty.*
2a. *He left before anyone noticed it.*
2b. **He left after anyone noticed it.*
3a. *I argued against taking any more.*
3b. **I argued in favor of taking any more.*

The NPIs are admissible because the clauses convey negative propositions: that she had no difficulty in doing it, that no one had noticed it, that I argued we (or whoever) should not take any more. They thrive like nightshade in such environments. No such negative propositions are conveyed by the [b] examples, which contain prepositions of opposite meaning: the NPIs are therefore inadmissible. *Without* and *before* sanction NPIs quite generally, but *against* does so only in the rather special sense it has here.

He left after anyone noticed it.
He was already to be gone,
even when you are talking to him.

He was playing dead. He wore two coins
in his eyes, a double monocle.
He had, it seems, prepaid his fare,

and said his last words when he first arrived,
which words were once upon a time
is there a man who was still here.

Joint coordination with *and* contrasts with the default distributive coordination:

1.   *Kim and Pat know Greek.*   [distributive]
2.   *Kim and Pat are a happy couple.*   [joint]

Example [1] is equivalent to *Kim knows Greek and Pat knows Greek*, but if we attempt to expand [2] in the same way the result is incoherent: **Kim is a happy couple and Pat is a happy couple.* The difference is that knowing Greek applies to Kim and Pat distributively, i.e., individually or separately, but being a happy couple does not—it is both Kim and Pat together, jointly, who are a happy couple. But *both* is excluded from joint coordination:

1.   *Both Kim and Pat are happy.*   [distributive]
2.   **Both Kim and Pat are a happy couple.*   [joint]

Both is also excluded from examples like *I want to see Kim and no-one else / Kim and only Kim,* where the second coordinate serves to exclude everyone other than Kim. *I want to see both Kim and not Kim* may affront logic, and perhaps cause other trouble, but, grammar will not forbid it.

Both Kim and Pat are a happy couple,
Kim with Pat and Pat with Kim,
though Kim and Kim will never meet,

nor Pat with Pat, unless the one
should stand in the other's bathroom mirror
and see herself reflected in

his eyes, or is that them, in theirs,
as who could ever hope to say
who hasn't met them all at once?

A subordinate clause characteristically functions as dependent within some larger construction. Comparative clauses form a subcategory of subordinate clauses, contrasting with relative and content clauses. The counterpart of a comparative phrase is normally omitted:

1.   *She is <u>older</u> than [I am ___].*
2.   *She went to <u>the</u> same <u>school</u> as [I went to ___].*

The comparative phrases are *older than I am* and *the same school as I went to*, and counterparts to these, corresponding phrases minus the comparative complement, i.e., *old* and *the school*, are understood but unexpressed in the comparative clause. We understand "I am *y* old," "I went to *y* school," but *old* and *school* must be left implicit as well as the *y* variables, for reasons of redundancy and sometimes of tact. The syntax thus excludes:

1.   * *She went to the same <u>school</u> as [I went to the <u>school</u>].*
2.   * *She is <u>older</u> than [I am <u>old</u>].*

She is older than I am old.
I am older than she was once
she counted up. The oldest is?

Don't answer yet. You'll need to know
how she is anger than I am awe,
how other she is than I am own,

but order by far than everyone else
am I, so tell me: how is that old?
For the answer, look in back of the book.

Universal quantification is expressed by a number of quantifiers, of which *all* is prototypical. Existential quantification indicates a quantity or number greater than zero. *Some* and *any* express existential quantification, and mark the noun phrase as indefinite (i.e., not specifying a definite quantity). Leaving aside the free choice sense of any (*any*$_f$), they are polarity-sensitive items, with *some* having a positive orientation, *any*$_n$ a negative orientation. Compare:

1a.   *We've got some milk.*
1b.   * *We've got any milk.*
2a.   * *We haven't got some milk.*
2b.   *We haven't got any milk.*

Any$_n$ is usually but by no means always unstressed. It can be stressed, for example, when it is the focus of negation: *I don't think* ANY *milk was spilt all night.* The stubbornly negative orientation of *any*$_n$ can be reinforced by the polarity-sensitive *at all* or *ever*: *He hadn't made any milk at all / ever.*

We've got any milk, but only any.
Was there one in particular you wanted?
Sadly, that's just the one we don't have.

Some of our milks are white and some
are perfectly clear and some are blue
in the bottle and vivid red in the glass.

Which of these many milks is for you?
Milk makes the man, but a man makes no milk.
He gets what he asks for all the same.

*MOOD

Each, unlike *every*, normally involves a discrete set. So, although a noun phrase like *each meeting* is itself indefinite, we understand that there is some definite set of meetings to which the quantification applies. This, however, is not necessarily so with noun phrases determined by *every*. Compare:

1a. *Last year each meeting was memorable.*
1b. *Last year every meeting was memorable.*
2a. *Each waiter is discreet.*
2b. *Every waiter is discreet.*
3a. **We lunch together each other day.*
3b. *We lunch together every other day.*

Example [1] speaks specifically about last year's meetings, so there must be an identifiable set of meetings involved. In contexts like this, *each* and *every* are equally appropriate. But the difference is clear in [2]. Here [2b] is interpreted generically: to be a waiter is to be discreet. Example [2a], however, doesn't have this generic interpretation: rather, we recognize some contextually identified set of waiters, each of whom is discreet, though there may be others who are not. With time (and other measure) expressions, the identifiable set requirement with *each* is not so evident, for we can have *We lunch together each day*, emphasizing the freshness, the promise of each occasion. Nevertheless, *every* occurs more freely in this kind of context, as is evident from the contrast in [3].

We lunch together each other day,
by custom at the Interwar,
but not today, I am afraid.

Too much, today, is already said.
One wishes it were otherwise.
Another day then? Any will do,

though yesterday would be ideal.
We'll lunch at noon by candlelight.
We loved each other, as did you.

Some determiners (words like articles or possessive pro-
nouns that help clarify what a noun refers to) combine with
both count and non-count singular nouns, as in *the houses*
and *the equipment*, *my gloves* and *my clothing*, and so on.
There are others, however, that are wholly or predominantly
restricted to one or other class of noun. For example, *a little*,
enough, *little*, *much*, and *sufficient* are incompatible with
count singular nouns, as illustrated in the following, where
the [a] examples are count, and the [b] are non-count.

1a.   *Why has he so <u>much</u> / <u>little</u> priest?*
1b.   *Why was there so <u>much</u> / <u>little</u> damage?*
2a.   *He damaged <u>a little</u> knee.*
2b.   *She drank <u>a little</u> water.*
3a.   *He has got <u>enough</u> / <u>sufficient</u> son.*
3b.   *He has got <u>enough</u> / <u>sufficient</u> strength.*

Example [2a] is of course grammatical with *little* an adjective
and *a* the indefinite article ("He damaged a small knee"): we
are concerned here with *a little* as determinative. With nouns
having both count and non-count senses, the occurrence of
one of these items selects a non-count interpretation: *There
isn't much water left*; *We need a little discipline*; *Is there enough
patience?* *A patience* will not be enough.

He damaged a little knee. It needs
a little time. It's hard to know
how much. Perhaps a little year,

perhaps a little more. It's hard
to know what's left, how much there was
to start. It wasn't an awful lot.

A little one, a little two,
a little grace, a little crook,
enough to kneel, with a little luck.

The range of semantic relations between the genitive noun phrase and the noun which is its head is vast, and largely parallel to that found between subject and predicate in clause structure.

1.	*Mary's green eyes*	*Mary has green eyes.* [d has body part h]
2.	*Mary's book*	*Mary writes a book.* [d is creator of h]
3.	*Mary's anger*	*Mary is angry.* [d has feeling h]
4.	*the flood's consequences*	*The flood has consequences.* [d has result h]

And so on. The genitive noun phrase often functions as a subject-determiner, specifying one instance among many candidates. Sometimes the subject-determiner genitive is interchangeable with an *of* phrase: *the flood's consequences* and *the consequences of the flood*, for example. Certain semantic relations, however, are excluded from the subject-determiner construction, but permitted in the *of* phrase one. These are illustrated in:

5.	*red wine's glass*	*the glass of red wine* [h is quantity of d]
6.	*unemployment's problem*	*the problem of unemployment* [h has content d]
7.	*the hay stack's painting*	*the painting of the hay stack* [h is depiction of d]
8.	*all battles' battle*	*the battle of all battles* [h is supreme example of d]

There is also no genitive counterpart of the predicative construction *that stupid nitwit of a husband* (cf. *a husband's stupid nitwit*).

The hay stack's painting hangs in the Met;
the painting, that is, of the hay stack, the one
by Monet, not the one by Van Gogh,

the rose-blue, snow-lit one with the stack
smack in the middle. It has the same deal
with many painters (e.g., Millet),

appearing not for a cut, nor a stake,
but rather for the sovereign right
to have your eyes back whenever it wants.

Adjectives that do not normally occur except as attributive modifiers, positioned before the nouns they modify, include:

damn	sole	lone	very
drunken	umpteenth	only	former
frigging	ersatz	self-same	main
future	latter	veritable	premier
marine	mock	eventual	soi-disant
mere	self-confessed	maiden	would-be
principal	utter	own	
putative	erstwhile	self-styled	

Ordinary attributive adjectives can be used predicatively with the same sense, but attributive-only adjectives cannot: thus we have *that damn noise*, but not **That noise is damn*; *a drunken sailor* but not **a sailor who was drunken*; and so on. There are some additional limits on the use of attributive-only adjectives. For example, their use with pronouns gives mixed results, particularly with *one*, a count noun. Compare:

1a.   *the <u>main</u> objections*
1b.   *the <u>main</u> ones*
2a.   *an <u>utter</u> disgrace*
2b.   **an <u>utter</u> one*

Such exclusions as [2b] are not systematic but they are none-theless veritable.

An utter one: how you can tell
is because it's been smoked down to the filter,
chewed to the tin ring around the eraser.

Everything tasty has that bit
you use to hold the rest of it with.
What's left to say now you're down to that?

—down to the socket, after you're finished
smiling, after you've spit the last smile
out of your mouth or after you've swallowed it.

There are some special constraints on expressions consisting of a preposition followed by a noun (sometimes preceded by *the* or *a*), followed in turn by a second preposition and a noun phrase, as in: *in accordance with, under the aegis of, on account of, in/on behalf of,* and so on. These differ in two respects from free expressions such as: *She put it* [*on her tab at the hotel*]. In the first place, they are in varying degrees idiomatic, so that the meaning of the whole is not derivable in a fully systematic way from the meanings of the components. Secondly, they do not permit the full range of syntactic manipulation that applies with free expressions—manipulations involving additions, omissions, and replacements. The most fossilized of such expressions, such as *in case of, by dint of, in lieu of, by means of, on pain of, in quest of, in search of, in spite of, in view of, by virtue of, by way of,* disallow all of these manipulations:

1.   *[*Dint of hard work*] *achieves wonders.*
2.   **She achieved this* [*by dint*].
3.   **She achieved this* [*by pure dint of hard work*].
4.   **She achieved this* [*by dints of hard work*].
5.   **She achieved this* [*by the dint of hard work*].
6.   **She achieved this* [*by hard work's dint*].

The less fossilized expressions allow one or a few changes, but none of them allows all.

1.   *I'm writing* [*in / on behalf of my son*].
2.   *I'm writing* [*in / on my son's behalf*].
3.   **I'm writing* [*in / on behalf*].

We speak only on the language's behalf.

I'm writing on behalf. My palm
is blue with ink. I'm trying to
keep up, writing as it befalls.

I hold the spoon by the silver bowl,
the fork by the tines; the shovel handle
I push pointlessly into the ground.

I'm writing on behalf. I hold
the pen tight by the wetter end:
see, I hold the dry end toward you.

*SOURCES

The sentences, clauses, or phrases that begin each of these poems are drawn mostly from Rodney Huddleston and Geoffrey K. Pullum's *The Cambridge Grammar of the English Language* (Cambridge: Cambridge University Press, 2002), and, in two instances, from Bernard Comrie's *Tense* (Cambridge: Cambridge University Press, 1985). On the pages facing the poems, I have adapted the discussions of the relevant topics in grammar that the asterisked sentences illustrate. Sometimes I have combined passages from my sources, and I have sorted them into categories (tense, agreement, case, gender, mood) that their authors might not fully endorse; sometimes I have perturbed their texts slightly. I have tried always to be faithful to their analysis and amenable to their difficulty. Errors with an asterisk are always reproduced verbatim. All other errors are my own, but everyone else's too if we want them.

*If it will rain tomorrow (C 46–48)
*He had had gone (C 77)
*The flag is being red (HP 119)
*I was recognizing her (HP 120–122)
*He was dying for an hour (HP 122)
*Either boy has a key (HP 387)
*Are you either coming or not (HP 1306)
*They resemble closely (HP 298, 302)
*John and his father amazes me (HP 507–508)
*How difficult problems (HP 919–20)
*I haven't any money on myself (HP 1488)
*This scissor will have to be sharpened (HP 342)
*The red other boxes (HP 1518)
*A loud explosion heard the children (HP 243–44)

*An asleep child (HP 57, 559)
*She doesn't know him already (HP 822)
*He left after anyone noticed it (HP 837)
*Both Kim and Pat are a happy couple
 (HP 1281, 1306)
*She is older than I am old (HP 1106, 1108)
*We've got any milk (HP 358–59, 380, 382)
*We lunch together each other day (HP 378)
*He damaged a little knee (HP 339)
*The hay stack's painting (HP 473–74, 477)
*An utter one (HP 553–55)
*I'm writing on behalf (HP 618–20)

Some of these poems have appeared previously in *The Paris Review* and *The Yale Review*.

Publications in this series include:

Jeff Dolven is a poet and a scholar of poetry in no particular order. His poems have appeared in *The Paris Review*, *The Yale Review*, *The New Yorker*, and elsewhere, and in a collection, *Speculative Music*; his books of criticism include *Senses of Style* and *In Other Words*. He teaches at Princeton University and is an editor-at-large at *Cabinet* magazine.

A New English Grammar
Jeff Dolven

Publisher: dispersed holdings
Editorial assistance: Leonard Nalencz

Graphic design: Nicholas Weltyk
Printing: Nocaut, Mexico City

First edition, 2022: 500 copies

dispersed holdings is Sal Randolph and David Richardson.
www.dispersedholdings.net

ISBN 979-8-9867990-0-1